I0060579

You've Been Arrested:
Now What?

Humbly dedicated to my beautiful, loving, and supportive family:
My parents, Nima & Juliana, Mona & Paul, and wonderful Amin

Parker Press Inc. created this publication to provide you with accurate information concerning the subject matter covered, for educational purposes. Parker Press Inc. does not render legal or other professional advice, and this publication is not a substitute for the advice of an attorney, nor does it constitute the rendering of legal or professional advice or services to a particular individual. If legal or other expert assistance is needed, the services of a qualified professional should be sought to address the specific needs in your situation.

Real Life Legal™ is a trademark registered in the U.S. Patent and Trademark Office.

Copying any portion of the original material presented in this book, or from the Real Life Legal™ website or placing it on any electronic media without the consent of Parker Press Inc. is prohibited by law and violators risk criminal penalties and monetary damages for copyright infringement.

Copyright © 2016 Parker Press Inc.

Parker Press Inc.
Briarcliff Manor, NY 10510

ISBN: 978-1-941760-06-2

For the latest information and updates to this material, check out:
http://www.reallifelegal.com/updates

You've Been Arrested:
Now What?

Maryam Jahedi, Esq.

Real Life Legal™

Helpful Guides for Everyday Legal Matters

Parker Press Inc.

Contents

Contents

What This Book's About

From your very first contact with police, you need to know your rights and what to expect. Getting a lawyer ASAP is the best thing you can do for yourself.

Coming in contact with the criminal justice system can happen to any of us and can be a confusing experience. If you understand the system and the process, from the very first contact with the police to facing the court and the charges brought against you, you're ahead of the game. It is equally as important to know your rights as an accused.

This book outlines the typical process the accused goes through when charged with a crime. It explores the rights of the accused, and the criminal process. If you are accused of a crime, you should always have a criminal lawyer represent you. A court will appoint a lawyer to represent you if you cannot afford one.

When it comes to criminal matters, certain types of cases occur more frequently than others. Some of the cases that have unique aspects are covered in more depth in this book. These include:

- Domestic violence.

- Youthful offenders.

- Driving while intoxicated/impaired or under the influence.

- Criminal matters involving non-U.S. citizens.

This book also includes information on how those convicted may gain some relief from the collateral damage caused by their convictions – if they meet certain standards. There are ways to petition for relief to regain rights, which may include sealing and expunging criminal records. The availability of this relief depends on the law of the state in which you were convicted.

Some Backstory: Criminal Law Basics

Each state has its own laws concerning what constitutes "crimes" or "offenses," and there are also federal laws which make certain activities crimes. Law enforcement, lawyers and the system all have a hand in what happens to an "accused."

Criminal law involves: (1) police and law enforcement which investigate crimes; (2) **"adjudication,"** which begins after arrest and moves an accused through the court system; and (3) the consequences of being convicted of a crime.

Criminal activities generally fall within three categories:

1. Offenses, such as jaywalking or littering, which typically are punishable by a fine.

2. Misdemeanors, which may carry a prison sentence of up to a year.

3. Felonies, which are more serious crimes, that carry a sentence of more than a year.

"Crimes" generally refers to misdemeanors and felonies where a defendant could serve jail time.

In the legal system, crimes are often categorized as crimes against the "person" and crimes against "property." The most serious crimes and the "degree" or "elements" of the crime depend on what occurred during the course of the criminal activity. Following are the most serious crimes:

- **Homicide:** When a person purposely, knowingly, recklessly or negligently causes the death of another person. A higher degree of the crime would be present if the death was intentionally, as opposed to negligently, caused.

- **Sexual Assault:** Forced sexual conduct without a victim's consent or when a victim is underage.

- **Robbery:** Unlawful taking, by force or threat of force, of property which is in someone's immediate possession.

- **Burglary:** Unlawful entry into a residence, building or vehicle, without consent, with intent to commit a felony or theft (larceny).

- **Larceny:** Unlawful taking or attempt to take property of another, without force or deceit, but with intent to permanently deprive the owner of his/her property.

Within one type of criminal activity, there can be both misdemeanor and felony charges. For example, petty larceny may be a misdemeanor if the amount stolen is less than $100. However, if the theft is of more valuable property, let's say a car worth $25,000, then the charge may be a felony. Within types of crimes, there can also be a "degree" of crime. For example, a robbery may be a "first-degree" felony if a weapon is used, but a lower degree if no weapon is used.

Each state has laws that define the elements of a crime. When it comes to prosecuting a criminal defendant in court, these elements of the crime must be proven beyond a reasonable doubt for the prosecutor to secure a conviction.

Accused of a Crime?

Whether you're innocent, guilty, or things just look bad, the minute you're an "accused," you have rights and it's essential to know them.

Popular fiction and crime dramas give many examples of how guilty and innocent people alike can come into contact with the criminal justice system. Know your rights when it comes to:

- Searches by law enforcement.

- Evidence seized with or without a warrant.

- Police stops without a warrant.

- Custody and arrest.

Knowing your rights and what is permitted and not permitted on the part of law enforcement can be critical in getting the best outcome for yourself if you find yourself entangled in a criminal matter.

Your Right to a Criminal Defense Attorney

The United States Constitution and the constitutions of each state guarantee the right to legal representation for individuals charged with a criminal offense. If you are charged with a criminal offense and cannot afford an attorney, the state is obligated to appoint one free of charge. *You have rights under the United States Constitution whether or not you are a citizen of the United States.*

Twelve Rules to Live By in the Criminal Justice System

Experience is the best teacher—but you don't have to personally have the experience to learn from it. Knowing some ground rules can make a big difference in what can happen.

The following twelve pieces of information can dramatically impact what happens to you once you are involved in a crime or accused of criminal activity:

1. **Ignorance of the Law Is Not an Excuse for Breaking the Law.** You could, unknowingly, be breaking a law even if the same action is legal in another state or even another country.

2. **When Miranda Rights Are Given.** If taken into police custody, even before the questioning begins (about the incident that led to your arrest) the police must tell you:

   a. Of your right to remain silent,

   b. That any statement you make may be used as evidence against you, and

   c. That you have the right to first speak with a lawyer and have a lawyer with you when being questioned. If criminal charges have not yet been brought against you, the government is not required to provide a free lawyer.

3. **How to Invoke Your Right to Remain Silent.** Anything you say, even if it seems harmless and unimportant, can be used against you in court. If arrested, you *do not* have to answer any questions. If you choose to refuse to answer questions, *affirmatively and clearly* state to the police that you wish to remain silent.

4. **You Can Ask for an Attorney at Any Point.** Even if you waive your Miranda rights and decide to answer the questions asked by the police, you have a right to stop the questioning at any time and to request an attorney be present, even in the middle of the questioning. It is never too late to ask for an attorney.

5. **The Court Will Appoint an Attorney if Needed.** If arrested and charged with a crime, you have the right to a criminal attorney even if you cannot afford one. The court will appoint a lawyer for you.

6. **If Police Contact You, Call an Attorney Before Speaking to Them.** If you are contacted by the police prior to an arrest being made and told you are subject to a criminal investigation or are simply told that the police have a few questions for you, call a lawyer immediately! A criminal attorney can best advise you regarding the risks and benefits of cooperating with the police.

7. **Don't Grant Entry Without a Search Warrant.** If police or FBI agents show up at your home without a search or arrest warrant, you are not obligated to allow them into your home or to search your property.

8. **Read the Warrant.** If police or FBI agents have an arrest or search warrant, you can still exercise the right to remain silent. The warrant must specify in detail the places to be searched and persons or items to be taken away. Tell the agents that you *would like to see the warrant* and that they *do not have your consent to the search.* This limits the police and does not authorize them to search beyond what is specified in the warrant.

9. **Do Not Lie.** Lying to or misleading the police is a criminal offense on its own. However, remaining silent is not a crime and is your constitutional right.

10. **Leave Your Stuff at Home.** If you anticipate being arrested or if you voluntarily appear at a precinct at the request of the police, leave your personal property at home. However, take at least two forms of identification with you and quarters for telephone calls.

11. **Know an Emergency Contact Phone Number by Heart.** Your cell phone will be confiscated after an arrest and you may not have access to your contacts.

12. **You're Innocent Until Proven Guilty.** Even after being arrested, you are presumed innocent until proven guilty. Guilt must be proven beyond a reasonable doubt in court for you to be convicted of a crime. Simply being subject to an arrest does not mean you have been convicted of a crime.

REAL LIFE EXAMPLE

Bob Thomas was arrested on the street late at night for selling cocaine to another person and was taken to the police station to be processed. While waiting, he was taken to a room by two officers and asked questions about the incident. Bob was asked how long he was dealing and who his provider of the controlled substance was.

Bob was aware of his right to remain silent while in police custody and refused to answer any questions, even when the police promised to let him go if he answered just those few questions. Bob *affirmatively* and *clearly* told the officers that he would not answer any questions and that he wished to speak with a lawyer. He also told the officers that he wished to have his attorney present while being questioned. By entertaining his rights to remain silent and have an attorney present, Bob made sure he did not make any statement which could later be used against him.

Your Arrest Mantra: Things to Remember if Arrested

- "I do not have to answer any questions."

- "I have the right to remain silent."

- "I would like to speak with an attorney."

- "I do not consent to have my house or my person searched."

Want to Know More About Your Constitutional Rights?

Here are some additional resources to learn more about your constitutional rights:

- http://www.law.cornell.edu/constitution/billofrights

- http://ccrjustice.org/

- http://www.archives.gov/exhibits/charters/bill_of_rights_transcript.html

Getting Arrested

Police have rules they must follow when making an arrest, starting with advising you of your Miranda rights. Here's what you can expect.

A criminal case usually starts when an arrest is made by a police officer or other law enforcement agent.

An officer may make arrests if the officer witnesses a criminal act being committed or if there is probable cause to believe a criminal act was committed. **"Probable cause"** is a level of reasonable belief, based on facts that can be articulated, that a criminal act was committed.

What Is a "Stop and Frisk?"

If an officer conducts a "stop and frisk," it does not mean you are arrested. A **"stop and frisk"** is when an officer who is suspicious of an individual stops and frisks (pats down) the person. The purpose of a frisk is only to make sure the person stopped is not dangerous and not armed. Unlike a full search after an arrest, a frisk is a pat-down of outer clothing in search of a weapon. If no weapon is found, the search should not go any further.

You Can Be Stopped Without a Warrant

The police do not need a warrant to stop you on the street. This can be the case if they believe a crime is underway and you are involved. Once the police stop you, you must remain. However, if they ask you questions you are not required to answer them. The police are not required to give you Miranda warnings if you have not been arrested. You may be asked for your name and ID card.

Clarify Whether You're "Under Arrest"

If you are unsure whether or not an arrest is taking place, ask the officer if you are under arrest. If you're not under arrest, you do not have to go with the officer to the police station, nor do you have to answer any questions. You can decline to answer and simply walk away.

If you are under arrest, the officer will put you in handcuffs and take you to the police station. At the time of arrest, the officer will tell you why you are being arrested, how the arrest is authorized, whether the officer has an arrest warrant or has reasonable cause to believe you committed a crime. If any of those are the case, the arrest is authorized and legal.

If your arrest is legal, the officer may conduct a search of you, your clothing and a limited search of the area close to you. If the arrest is done illegally, the issue of the arrest and what is found on you would be addressed in court.

Miranda Warnings are Mandatory

Once arrested and in police custody, the police must give you Miranda warnings before any interrogation or questioning. The police may not use physical violence, threats or false promises in their interrogation to get you to waive your Miranda rights. Nor can they use those tactics to get you to answer questions, even if you have waived your right to remain silent.

Identification Procedures

When you are in custody, if your identification as a criminal is at issue, the police might arrange for an identification procedure by the victim, a witness to the crime or an undercover police officer. The identification procedure might take place in form of a photo array, line-ups (as commonly seen on TV) or a show-up.

White-Collar Crime

"White-collar crime" typically refers to nonviolent, financially motivated crimes committed by government or business professionals. Examples of such crimes include bribery, money laundering, fraud, or identity theft. In white collar cases, an arrest is more likely to be made by state or federal authorities and subject to an arrest warrant signed by a judge. With the arrest warrant, an arrest can take place anywhere (e.g., your home, place of employment or on the street).

In some states, the accused has a right to have his/her attorney present at the time of the identification procedure.

The police are not required to give you Miranda warnings if you are not under arrest —but they may still question you.

The Search

The U.S. Constitution protects against "unreasonable searches and seizures." But what exactly is unreasonable?

The law for arrest and the taking of physical evidence falls within the Fourth Amendment of the United States Constitution, which protects individuals against "unreasonable searches and seizures" by the police or government agents.

Stop and Search on the Street/ In a Public Place

The police can stop and search you on the street, or in any public place, if they have probable cause for arrest. Probable cause provides a basis for the police to stop and search you.

However, the following alone do not constitute a basis for the police to stop and search:

- Presence in a high-crime area.

- Being in the company of someone police suspect has committed a crime.

- Being known to have previous convictions.

- Your age, race or gender.

A police officer or FBI agent can search you if you consent to the search. However, without your consent, a search can only be conducted with a valid search warrant or if you are being placed under arrest.

Sam, wearing a hoodie and a backpack, was walking fast on the street late at night. A police officer approached and asked him to stop for a minute. The officer asked Sam his name and his business walking on the street that late at night. He responded with his name and that he was on his way to a friend's house. The officer looked at Sam's bag and asked if he could do a quick search of what was in it.

Sam, thinking he had to consent to the search, gave his bag to the officer. After looking inside, the officer found 50 grams of cocaine and placed Sam under arrest for possession of a controlled substance. At Sam's hearing, his lawyer argued that the arrest was illegal as Sam was stopped by the police without an arrest warrant or without the officer having reasonably believed that Sam had committed a crime. As the arrest was found to be illegal, the cocaine which was found was suppressed, which meant it was not allowed to be used as evidence against Sam. As a result, the charges against him were dismissed.

Home Search

The U.S. Constitution gives all of us a greater right to privacy in our own homes than anywhere else. As a result of this protection, the police generally cannot enter your home and conduct a search without: (1) your consent or, (2) an arrest/search warrant.

The police may enter a suspect's home without a warrant or consent when there are sufficient exigent circumstances that would justify the entry. These can include:

- Emergency situations to aid a person inside the home in distress and danger.

- Cases of hot pursuit and chase of a suspect who enters the home.

- When the purpose of entry is to prevent destruction of evidence of the crime, which is believed to be in the home.

In cases where there is no emergency and the police know the identity of the suspect and have probable cause to arrest, the police should apply for an arrest warrant from the court before going to the suspect's home for arrest.

Police should show you a copy of the arrest warrant if they show up at your door with one. If they don't show it to you, ask to see it!

An **"arrest warrant"** is a document signed by a judge or a judicial magistrate that allows the police to arrest a person. To obtain an arrest warrant, officers must present to the magistrate or the judge enough facts to constitute probable cause for the arrest.

Automobile Stop and Search

In order to stop your car, the police must have probable cause to believe you have committed a traffic law violation. If there is a traffic violation the stop would be lawful, and the duration of the stop should be reasonable in relation to the traffic violation. For a traffic violation alone, the police cannot do a search of your car. For example, if you are stopped for a traffic violation and the police ask you to provide documentation (e.g., registration and driver's license), the police officer cannot direct you to empty your glove compartment and then search the contents. That would be considered an impermissible search of your vehicle.

On the other hand, if you are being arrested for committing a crime, a search of your car in conjunction with your arrest is allowed if there is reason for the police to believe that evidence relevant to the arrest might be found in the car.

REAL LIFE EXAMPLE

Richard was driving home from work very late at night. He noticed a police car behind him with lights and sirens on, pulled his car over and waited in the car until the police approached him. The policeman told Richard he had been stopped because he had run a red light at a previous intersection. The policeman asked Richard for his license and registration and Richard started looking in his glove compartment for the documents.

The officer, while waiting, asked Richard to open the trunk of the car so that he could take a quick look inside. Since the officer had no reason to believe Richard committed a crime, the search of his trunk violated his Fourth Amendment Rights against unconstitutional search and seizure. If Richard had been carrying illegal firearms in his trunk, the evidence of the search (the firearms) would be suppressed (prevented) as evidence in court. Stopping Richard's car was a valid stop due to the traffic violation, but the search of the trunk would not be.

Get a Criminal Attorney ASAP If Arrested

The criminal justice system is one place you don't want to "do it yourself." A lot can go wrong and a lot is at stake. Get a lawyer to help you navigate your rights and the system.

It is essential to contact a criminal attorney as soon as you find out that you or a loved one is arrested and charged with a crime. A well-trained, experienced and devoted criminal attorney will lead you through the complexities of the criminal justice system and make sure your rights are defended and protected.

Having a criminal record can permanently and negatively affect your life and livelihood. It's essential to have a criminal attorney represent you as soon as possible—to obtain the best result possible when facing arrest.

What Does a Criminal Attorney Do?

A criminal attorney who knows the law and how the system works helps you navigate the process and protect your rights. Criminal attorneys can:

- Explain the charges brought against you.

- Explain the potential sentences if convicted.

- Discuss your options with you.

- Communicate on your behalf with the District Attorney:

  - To see if a lesser charge is offered/available.

  - To negotiate alternative measures in order to avoid a criminal record.

- Explain the legal documents and walk you through the criminal procedure.

- Defend you at your criminal trial.

The sooner you discuss your situation with a criminal attorney, the better it is for you. The attorney can then act quickly on your behalf, to not only protect your rights, but to make sure any evidence that could help your case is preserved. Attorney involvement also sends a message to law enforcement to not overstep their authority under the law.

If you are unable to afford an attorney for your criminal case, the judge will appoint you a court appointed attorney (one whose fees are paid by the court).

The Criminal Process —Arrest to Appeal

Once you've been arrested, you're in the "system" of police and judicial protocols. Knowing what to expect, understanding your rights and having your attorney advise you are essential for the best outcome.

The Arrest

If you are arrested, you should only give statements on advice of your attorney. Know and understand your Miranda rights! Your emotions and your ego may push you to make statements to explain your side of the story, but any statement you give the police could do you harm and should only be made in the presence of an attorney.

Any statement given to the police at the time of an arrest can do harm and should not be made without the advice and the presence of an attorney.

At the Precinct

After an arrest, you will be taken to the police station in the precinct where the arrest occurred and where you will go through booking procedures, including fingerprinting and paperwork. A police officer will ask your name, address, date of birth and your social security number.

The booking and intake process and paperwork preparation can take anywhere from four to six hours, during which time you are held in a cell. Your personal property, including your cell phone, will be removed from your possession.

Once you are interviewed, fingerprinted and your photo is taken, you will be led to central booking (holding cells located at the

Police Conduct/ Activities After Arresting a Suspect

- If you have been lawfully arrested, the police are permitted to search you, as well as the area under your immediate control. This is sometimes called a "grab area" and includes the glove compartment of your car if you are arrested in your car.

- The police are not allowed to use excess force or brutality during the course of an arrest; however, if you resist, the police can use "reasonable" force to proceed with the arrest and prevent you from injuring yourself or them.

courthouse). You will wait there until processed (which could take several hours) and then appear for the first time before a judge. This first appearance before a judge is called an **"arraignment."**

Prior to the arraignment and while in central booking, you will be given an opportunity to speak with a lawyer. If you have not already contacted a lawyer, or can't afford one, the court will appoint a public defender (appointed counsel is free of charge) to interview you before the arraignment.

Even though the public defender attorney is appointed by the court, he/she is your attorney and whatever you say to the attorney is confidential and privileged.

In unusual cases, after the intake procedure at the precinct, the police might issue you a **"Desk Appearance Ticket (DAT),"** which will allow you to leave the precinct but require you to return to court on a specific date for arraignment of the charges. DATs are issued at the discretion of the police and in less extreme cases of disorderly conduct or minor crimes.

Central Booking

If a DAT is not issued, you are taken to local central booking which is usually inside or adjacent to the criminal court building. When your case is ready to be heard in court, you will be transferred to a holding pen adjacent to the arraignment courtroom.

Booking Process Tips

- It is important to remain calm and cooperative while the booking and intake questions and procedures are taking place.

- This process may take several hours and your cooperation will make the process go more smoothly.

- The police will take away your cell phone so make sure you have emergency contact numbers memorized to reach someone you trust to get you a lawyer.

If English is not your native language and you have trouble communicating with your attorney in English, an interpreter will be provided by the court to assist in your attorney interview.

Interview with a Justice Agency

While at central booking, you may be interviewed by a justice agency representative who will evaluate your work, family and community ties. This agency, which is independent of the court system, will present a recommendation regarding your release, and whether or not bail should be set. The agency representative will generally ask about your work and family history and for the names and contacts of persons who could confirm what you have told the agency.

Interview with Your Lawyer

While at central booking, you will be given an opportunity to speak privately with an attorney or appointed counsel before appearing in front of a judge for your first appearance. Be frank with your attorney and give as much information as you think might be helpful. The point of this interview is to provide any information which can be used by the attorney to get you released.

Important details to share with your attorney:

- Any injuries as a result of the arrest or the incident.

- Any statements made to the police when arrested.

- Citizenship status.

- Any personal property confiscated when arrested.

- Names of family members or relatives and any contact information (so that the attorney can call on your behalf).

- Names of any witnesses to the incident.

Arraignment

An **"arraignment"** is the first appearance before a judge, where you are told of the charges brought against you. You will be present at your arraignment along with:

- The judge.

- Your lawyer.

- The prosecutor (a.k.a. District Attorney).

- Court reporter.

- Interpreter (if needed).

- Police officers to escort you.

- Correction officers if you are not released on bail.

At the arraignment, the District Attorney or prosecutor will either consent to your release without bail (which is unlikely) or will make recommendation as to why bail is appropriate. If the District Attorney asks for bail to be set, your attorney will argue for your release and will outline factors in support of release.

What Is Bail?

"Bail" is security to guarantee a criminal defendant will return to court for his/her next court date if released from jail while the case is still pending. Payment of bail is made by cash or bond. The amount set is suggested by the District Attorney but decided by the judge at arraignment.

Normally, cash bail is lower than a bond bail. A bond is guaranteed by another person's assets, e.g., home or valuable property, to insure that the person facing the charges will return to court for future court dates. The assets that support the bond will be forfeited if the person fails to show up for future court dates.

Factors Considered In Determining Bail

- Type and seriousness of the pending criminal charges.

- Your family and community ties, and length of residency in the community.

- Your employment history.

- Your criminal history and prior convictions, if any.

- Your previous records of responding to court appearances when required of you.

- Family members who are members of the same community. Also, it will help your bail application to have immediate family members present in court to show your strong family and community ties.

- The weight of evidence against you in the case.

- The sentence imposed if convicted.

Another way to post bail is called a "**surety bond**." Here, a bail bond company (licensed insurance company) posts the bail amount on behalf of the accused in return for a fee. The bail amount is forfeited if the accused does not appear, in which case the bail amount is owed in full to the bail bond company.

Make sure you carefully research a bail bond company to make sure it is licensed and regulated by the State's Insurance Department. You want to make sure the company is "legitimate" before you choose it to post bond. There are many companies and individuals who prey on the stress and fear that accompany being held in prison. Basic research can help you avoid a scam.

At this point the goal is to either:
(1) be released on your own recognizance
(ROR)—meaning you are released without
bail, and promise to make
your future court appearance; or,
(2) be released on a set bail.

How Is Bail Decided?

At your arraignment there are factors that the judge will consider in deciding whether to allow you to be released without bail, or to decide what amount to set for bail. The court will want to assess whether you are a flight risk, the likelihood that you will return for your future court dates while the case is pending and not be a danger to society if released.

Whether you have been released on bail or on your own recognizance (a.k.a ROR), **"Failure to appear (FTA)"** at a future court date is a crime of its own and is called "bail jumping." It could result in a what's known as a **"bench warrant"** being issued for your arrest, which means you could be arrested immediately on sight. A bench warrant is a type of arrest warrant, signed by a judge, authorizing your arrest for failing to show up at your scheduled court date. Always make sure you record future court dates somewhere and show up for your court dates.

Post-arraignment and Pre-trial Proceedings

Unless you plead guilty at arraignment, the case will be scheduled for future pre-trial hearings and for trial, in which case you and your lawyer will start preparing your case. As part of the preparation, your lawyer will request and receive discovery materials from the District Attorney. In addition, your lawyer will start an investigation and file appropriate motions for issues that arise as he/she learns more about your case.

Discovery materials can include (but are not limited to):

- Statements made by witnesses, by police officers or by medical personnel.

- Descriptions of your clothing and/or physical condition at the time of the arrest.

- Description of property recovered from you or at the scene.

- 911 call recordings or police radio calls.

- Pictures or videos taken from the scene of the crime.

- Any other details concerning the alleged crime.

Missed Your Court Date?

If you have missed a court date and believe a bench warrant has been issued against you, talk to your lawyer and have your lawyer accompany you to court to clear the warrant without being arrested.

- It will be helpful to bring any documentation explaining why you missed the court date.

- If you are not sure there is a warrant against you, call the clerk of the court (contact information is on the court's website) and ask if there is a warrant under your name.

Before the trial, the court will hear any pre-trial motions or arguments concerning suppression of evidence or evidentiary issues that one side or the other anticipates will arise at trial. A **"motion to suppress evidence"** seeks to prevent evidence from being used against you in court if it was obtained improperly by law enforcement during the course of your arrest.

Successful motions to suppress mean the evidence is limited or cannot be used against you at trial.

In the pre-trial phase, the court will also try to resolve any factual issues your attorney and the District Attorney do not agree on. This is undertaken by holding hearings for physical or testimonial evidence regarding the facts. The pre-trial issues can sometimes be found in your favor and sometimes against you.

If your case is not resolved by dismissal or you do not agree to plead guilty, it will eventually proceed to trial. The results of what happens at the pre-trial stage will apply to the trial. For example, if evidence is suppressed at pre-trial, it will be suppressed at the actual trial.

Plea Bargaining

"Plea bargaining" is a process where the criminal defendant and the prosecutor reach a compromise. Plea bargaining usually starts with an offer from the District Attorney, sometimes presenting a lower charge with a shorter sentence as incentive for the accused.

The decision to plead or not is ONLY in your hands and not your lawyer's. Your lawyer is obligated to convey to you any plea offer the District Attorney presents, and to explain to you the offense to which you are pleading as well as the minimum and maximum possible penalties.

Plea negotiations are very common in criminal cases. The purpose is to resolve the case faster than if the case went through the entire court process.

If an acceptable plea deal is reached, your lawyer will inform the court, on the record, that you would like to enter a plea of guilty. To accept the guilty plea, the court has its own specific procedures. The judge should, on the record, inform you of the rights you are giving up by pleading guilty, e.g., right to a trial, to remain silent, or to confront the witness accusing you. The judge also has to ensure your plea is made by you knowingly and voluntarily. A sentence hearing will follow, after the plea hearing or at a future date.

REAL LIFE EXAMPLE

David got into a fight while at a bar having drinks with his friends. The police arrived and arrested him. Later, he was charged with assault, harassment, and disorderly conduct. At his arraignment and with the advice of his attorney, David didn't plead to any of the charges and the case was adjourned for a pre-trial hearing. Meanwhile, his attorney negotiated with the prosecutor to allow David, as a first-time offender, to plead to the lowest charge on the complaint, which was the disorderly conduct and thus not a crime but a violation.

The prosecutor accepted the plea, conditional on David attending several weeks of anger management classes. After discussing the offer with his attorney, David pled to the disorderly conduct charge and was sentenced by the judge to the behavioral classes. Because he successfully completed the anger management classes, David avoided having a criminal conviction on his record.

What Happens At Trial?

If your case is not dismissed, and you haven't reached a plea bargain or pled guilty, your case will go to trial.

If your case is not resolved or dismissed at a pre-trial stage, it will be put on the court's calendar for trial. There are two types of trials: a bench trial (in which there is no jury and the case is presented before a judge) and a jury trial (in which your case is presented before a jury of six to twelve people).

A criminal trial is basically a formal examination of the evidence to determine whether you are guilty beyond a reasonable doubt of the charges against you. **"Beyond a reasonable doubt"** is the standard used in criminal trials to prove guilt and it is the toughest standard of proof.

A criminal defendant has a right to a jury trial under the U.S. Constitution, but also has the right to waive the right to a jury trial and have only a judge decide the case. In most states, the right to jury trial is granted in all felony cases and in more serious misdemeanors.

Jury Selection

Jury selection is the first step in the trial. Here, your attorney, the judge and the prosecutor question a pool of jurors to determine whether or not the jurors can be fair and impartial in making a decision after hearing the evidence in your case. Typically, if you are charged with a felony, your jury would consist of twelve people; if charged with a Class A misdemeanor, your jury would only consist of six people.

As part of jury selection, both you and the prosecutor have an opportunity to question and disqualify a juror from sitting on your jury. Disqualification generally occurs if either side believes the juror is legally unfit to serve because of bias or prejudice. This disqualification of the juror from jury panel is called **"challenge for cause."**

Both sides may also disqualify a fixed number of jurors for non-stated reasons, called **"peremptory challenges"** in jury selection.

Opening Statements

After the jury panel is selected, the judge will provide the jury with instructions about their duties, trial procedure and basic principles of law. After jury instructions are given, both sides give an opening statement that explains what the case is about and what evidence will be presented.

Your attorney may make an opening statement or choose not to do so. This is because under the Constitution, when accused of a crime, you have the right to remain silent and let the prosecutor prove the case. In most cases, however, the accused attorney does make an opening statement.

Direct and Cross Examination

After the opening statements are given, the prosecutor presents evidence. If there are witnesses, the prosecutor would put the witnesses on the stand and ask them questions to present to the jury what happened. This is called a **"direct examination."**

After the direct examination, your attorney has a chance to question the witness to prove that the witness is lying or to reduce the credibility of the witness or evidence. This is called **"cross examination."**

After the prosecution presents its evidence, your attorney may move to dismiss the charges based on insufficient evidence. If the motion is denied, your attorney then presents your case through evidence and witnesses, which can then be cross-examined by the prosecutor.

Creating Reasonable Doubt

The goal of the prosecution's presentation of evidence and witnesses is to prove beyond a reasonable doubt that an accused committed the crime for which he/she is charged. The defendant's attorney must create "reasonable doubt" by refuting the evidence, casting doubt on the prosecution's theory or presenting evidence to support the defendant's innocence.

You, as someone charged with an offense, have the right to testify or remain silent. The decision to testify or not is dependent on your specific case and should be discussed with your attorney.

A court stenographer records every single word said at the proceeding to create a transcript and record that may be needed for an appeal. The stenographer generally sits between the judge and the attorneys.

Closing Arguments

After the presentation of all the evidence from both sides, both parties give closing arguments. Closing arguments are the last opportunity for either party to address the jury. They are made on the basis of already presented evidence, and are intended to, for the last time, persuade the jury on the case.

Jury Deliberation and Verdict

After closing arguments are finished, the judge instructs the jury on the law and explains to them the legal concepts and elements of the crime you are charged with. The judge also explains to the jury what they need to find, based on the evidence, in order to find you guilty or not guilty of the charges. The jury is then taken to a private room to make a decision in the case; the process is called **"deliberation."**

During deliberation, the jury considers the evidence presented by both sides and determines whether or not the prosecutor has proven guilt beyond a reasonable doubt.

- The deliberation could take a few hours or a few days, and basically takes as long as needed until a verdict is reached.

- At any time during the deliberation, the jury might ask the judge to clarify any questions they might have, ask for more instructions on a specific charge or issue, or ask to review any evidence.

The "Double Jeopardy" clause in the Fifth Amendment to the U.S. Constitution prohibits anyone from being prosecuted twice for the same crime. If you are found not guilty, you cannot be re-prosecuted for the same crime.

What is a "Hung Jury?"

If the jury decides that the evidence presented proves your guilt beyond a reasonable doubt, the verdict is "guilty" and the case would be adjourned for sentencing. If the jury decides the evidence does not prove guilt beyond a reasonable doubt, the verdict is "not guilty," and you would be free to go.

A **"hung jury"** occurs if the jury cannot reach a verdict for any reason. The judge would declare a mistrial and the prosecution would decide whether or not to retry the case or drop the charges. If the prosecution decides to retry the case, a brand new jury panel is selected for the new trial.

Sentencing

If a guilty verdict is reached, your case is adjourned for sentencing. The sentence received depends on a variety of factors, including:

- Seriousness of the crime.

- Mitigating circumstances.

- Personal background and history.

- Repeat offender or youthful offender status.

Depending on the crime, criminal sentences can include: imprisonment, probation, fine, conditional or unconditional discharge, community service, restitution or attending behavioral programs.

Appeal

After sentencing, you have a right to appeal. An **"appeal"** is a request to a higher (appellate) court to review and change the decision of a lower court. The defendant may challenge the conviction itself or the sentence (without attacking the underlying conviction). A successful appeal usually restores a case to the initial stages, but can sometimes end the case altogether (such as when the appellate court finds that there's insufficient evidence to retry the defendant).

In cases where you plead guilty, you may have waived your right to appeal certain issues of the case. Ultimately, it is your decision, not your attorney's decision, to appeal. If you decide to appeal, there is a process your attorney will have to follow in order to file for an appeal.

Unanimous Verdicts Required in All But Two States

All U.S. states, except Oregon and Louisiana, require a unanimous jury verdict in a criminal case. This means that:

- Every single member of the jury must find the defendant guilty in order to have a guilty verdict.

- There is no "majority rule" in a jury trial in the other 48 states.

- If every member cannot reach the same answer, then the result would be called a "hung jury."

Domestic Violence

Domestic violence is a catch-all term for violence that occurs between people who are related or who have a social relationship.

It should come as no surprise that domestic violence can occur between people who are:

- Married, living together or even just dating.

- Heterosexual, lesbian or gay.

Charges for domestic violence cases include, but are not limited to, harassment, assault, sexual abuse, stalking, menacing or disorderly conduct.

State criminal courts now have specific divisions designated to and specializing in domestic violence cases. Many states pursue domestic violence cases aggressively to:

- Reduce recurrences.

- Reduce violence against women.

- Enforce policies of no tolerance for domestic violence/ violence behind closed doors.

While anyone can become a domestic violence perpetrator or victim, serious injuries resulting from domestic violence typically result from males attacking females. Though murder and rape can be considered forms of domestic violence, most often domestic violence consists of lesser forms of physical abuse such as slapping and pushing. Stalking can also be considered domestic violence.

If you are accused of domestic violence, it's essential to get an experienced criminal defense attorney to represent you.

Police Involvement in Domestic Violence

Domestic violence cases usually start with one of the parties calling the police after a fight breaks out. When police arrive, they interview both parties separately and prepare a family incident report. Depending on the severity of the situation and any injuries to the person making the complaint, the police might arrest the abuser and take him to the precinct to be processed.

In some cases, the incident is not reported to the police for hours or days after the incident. The police then might obtain an arrest warrant or contact the abuser and ask him or her to voluntarily surrender.

The police provide the case paperwork to the prosecutor's office. After reading the reports and allegations, and after speaking with the complaining witness (who is both a witness and a victim of the crime), the prosecutor decides whether to pursue the matter further by filing a criminal complaint in court.

Orders of Protection and Restraining Orders

An **"order of protection"** (also known as a restraining order) is a court-issued order to protect the safety of the complainant (or a witness) and lists behavior and actions the person named is forbidden from doing. The complainant might be a spouse, a girlfriend, a family member, a victim of sexual offense or any other person who is the victim of a specific offense.

These orders (often issued in domestic violence cases, in sexual offenses, in stalking cases or in assault cases) forbid an accused from:

- Contacting the complainant.

- Going near the complainant's home, place of work, or school.

- Doing anything to threaten or harass the complainant.

A person can get a criminal order of protection by first filing a complaint with the police. A person might file a complaint because of physical or mental abuse, assault, stalking or threatening.

Temporary Orders of Protection

After arraignment and in cases where a complaining witness is involved, a **"Temporary Order of Protection (TOP),"** which limits contact with the complaining witness as a condition of release or bail, may be issued. Under no circumstances should you violate the terms and conditions mentioned in the TOP because the consequences will make matters worse. A violation of a TOP may cause:

- A new arrest for violation of a court order.

- Rescission of bail requiring immediate imprisonment.

At the request of the complaining witness, the judge may agree to vary the terms of an order of protection or in rare cases, not issue one at all. To vary the terms of an order of protection, the judge may look into factors such as prior criminal history or prior violations of orders of protection, past allegations of domestic violence or physical abuse, and specific facts about the incident (like children present at the family home).

Prosecutors Decide on Domestic Violence Cases

The prosecutor's office decides whether or not to prosecute the case. This is true even in cases where the complaining witness changes her mind and wants to withdraw the complaint. If the prosecutor decides the case is serious enough to prosecute, the case will move forward.

The order of protection is generally a temporary order which remains in effect while the criminal case is pending. At the next court date, the clerk of the court may be instructed to issue a new order with a new expiration date. A permanent final order of protection may be issued or the temporary order of protection will be canceled when the criminal case is done.

For lawfully admitted non-U.S. citizens, violating an order of protection issued in relation to a domestic offense could also have negative immigration consequences. Violations of orders of protection in domestic cases are grounds for deportation.

If you are an alleged abuser subject to a TOP, and the complaining witness contacts you (by phone or text or email), ignore the contacts! And make sure you record the time and place of the contacts and let your attorney know about them.

Juveniles in the Criminal Justice Process

"Juvenile delinquency" is a term referring to a child committing an act that is considered a crime if committed by an adult.

In most states, a child is considered a person under the age of eighteen. Such cases are generally dealt with in the family court instead of criminal courts. Again, this is a matter of the law in the state where you reside or where the case is pending.

After a youth is arrested, the police may release the person after issuing him a Desk Appearance Ticket (DAT) to appear in court on a later date. The police may also choose to bring the child to court to appear before a judge if court is in session. If the court is closed, the police might take the child to a detention center until court reopens.

No statement can be taken from a juvenile while in custody unless his/her parent or guardian is present at the police station.

While in court, a probation intake officer will:

- Interview the child about the alleged crime.

- Ask questions about the child's living arrangements and school.

- Interview the child's parents.

- Interview the arresting officer and the complainant, if any.

After the interview, the intake officer determines whether the case should be prosecuted or, instead, dealt with through alternative means, such as restitution, community service, letter of apology or referral to other community-based involvement.

If the intake officer decides the case could not be resolved by alternative means, he will refer the case to the state's court having jurisdiction over these types of matters.

In juvenile offender proceedings, an intake officer generally prepares a report which assesses the risk the child will reoffend or fail to appear for the court date, if released. Based on that assessment, the decision whether to **"parole"** (release) the child or **"remand"** (hold) the child in detention is made. There is no bail in juvenile delinquency cases.

Does a Juvenile Offender Need a Lawyer?

A child accused of a crime needs a lawyer! If the child's parent or guardian cannot afford an attorney, the court will assign an attorney to represent the child. This lawyer, in most states, is referred to as "attorney for the child" and would have experience both in criminal and family matters.

Court Appearances for Youthful Offenders

Just as in any other case, the first appearance in court and before a judge is called an arraignment. Here, the child pleads guilty or not guilty and asks for a trial. A trial for a juvenile delinquency case is more of a fact-finding hearing before a judge than a full-blown jury trial. If the child is detained while the case is pending, he is entitled to a probable cause hearing first, which determines whether there is sufficient reason to hold the child in detention.

Types of Hearings

A "hearing" is a proceeding before a court or other decision-making body where evidence is heard and/or an issue as to law or fact is decided. There are many types of hearings in the legal system. At the fact-finding hearing, the parties present evidence and witnesses and each side has an opportunity to cross-examine the other party's witnesses. If the case against the child is proven beyond a reasonable doubt, the judge may find that the child committed some or all of the acts of which he/she is accused and a dispositional hearing (like an adult's sentencing hearing) is scheduled. If the case is not proven beyond a reasonable doubt, the judge will dismiss the case.

Sentencing of Juvenile Offenders

At a dispositional hearing, evidence and documentation are presented to the judge. This includes information on the child's home and school behavior, other court cases the child is involved in, and in some cases, mental health evaluation reports. The documentation included is any information relevant to helping the judge decide whether the child is in need of supervision, treatment or placement in detention.

This comprehensive report including court recommendations is prepared by a probation officer at the state's Department of Probation or Correction. Each state has a similar department/division which handles these matters. Before making a decision, the judge might also ask the child or the child's parents or guardians to testify.

Adjournment in Contemplation of Dismissal

"Adjournment in Contemplation of Dismissal" enables a judge to set certain conditions for the child to follow. If the child completes the conditions and does not get re-arrested, the case is dismissed. This decision of the judge is considered an order of the court.

If the child fails to follow the conditions stated in the order, he will be found in violation of probation. If there is a violation, the judge can revoke the disposition to dismiss the case since the conditions of

Sentencing for Juvenile Offenders

Punishment for youthful offenders is a matter of state law. Following are typical punishments:

- The child remains at home with no court supervision, but subjected to certain conditions such as drug testing.

- The child remains living at home, but is subject to supervision of court by the state's Department of Probation or similar division.

- The child is required to perform specified hours of community service or attend a community program designed for juveniles.

- The child is placed in a juvenile incarceration facility.

dismissal were not followed. The judge could then order a harsher disposition, including confinement in juvenile detention center.

Even if a child is found guilty of committing the act, a judge may rule that the child does not need confinement, supervision or treatment, and/or may adjourn/dismiss the case if/when certain conditions are met.

Driving While Intoxicated or Under the Influence (DWI or DUI)

Drunk driving is a leading cause of deaths in the U.S. and the criminal justice system increasingly has a zero tolerance and severe penalties for DWI or DUI. You won't just lose your license for a few weeks.

Being arrested for or convicted of **"driving while intoxicated (DWI)"** or **"driving under the influence (DUI)"** can have severe life-altering consequences, the least of which may be losing driving privileges while the case is pending. In recent years, states have clamped down on offenders and if you are charged with DWI or DUI, it is essential to speak with a criminal defense attorney to represent you.

You can be arrested and charged for a DWI/DUI even if you are not driving a vehicle. Sitting behind the wheel with the keys in the ignition is enough to be charged because technically, you are physically in control of the vehicle.

REAL LIFE EXAMPLE

Sally went out for dinner with few friends and had a few drinks at dinner, forgetting she had driven to the restaurant. After dinner, Sally thought she would sit in the car in the parking lot and wait until she sobered up to drive home. She started the car to turn on the heater, rested her head on the steering wheel and listened to music while sobering up. A police officer passing by her car became suspicious, approached Sally and arrested her for drunk driving. Because Sally appeared intoxicated while sitting behind the wheel of her car, this provided the officer probable cause to approach and make an arrest. An officer has to have probable cause for arrest or to stop a car.

If you are arrested for suspicion of DWI or DUI, your arrest follows the same procedures as arrests for any other crime. Possible reasons for your arrest could be that you provided a breath, blood or urine test which indicated your BAC (blood alcohol content) level was over the legal limit, had a field sobriety test done which showed signs of intoxication, or you simply refused all tests. Each state has its own laws in this regard, but they are similar.

Sobriety Tests

Chemical tests such as blood, urine and/or breath tests are administered to determine your blood alcohol content level. Field sobriety tests are balance and coordination exercises to show signs of intoxication and they are generally simple, like following a light with your eyes or walking a straight line.

Most state laws mandate that the officer who stops you for DUI or DWI must give you proper warnings of the consequences for refusing to submit to chemical tests. The warning typically requires the officer to let you know that your refusal will result in an immediate suspension and subsequent revocation of your license, whether or not you are convicted of the charges, and that a refusal can be used as evidence against you in court.

REAL LIFE EXAMPLE

Ian was driving home after watching a baseball game with friends and drinking. He had doubts about his ability to drive but drove himself home anyway. On the way, he was pulled over by a police officer who informed Ian his taillight had burned out. While talking to him about his light, the officer noticed Ian had difficulty answering simple questions and had slurred speech. When the officer asked Ian if he had been drinking, Ian answered, "Only a few beers," and proceeded to fail the sobriety test and breathalyzer test. He was then arrested for suspicion of drunk driving. In this scenario, stopping Ian was considered proper because driving with a burned taillight is a driving violation. Since the officer stopped Ian properly, his later arrest for suspicion of drunk driving was also deemed proper.

In most states, if you refuse to submit to chemical tests, you can be arrested and charged even without any test results, and your refusal can be used in court against you. While there may be less evidence to use against you to convict, in most states there is still a license suspension requirement due to the refusal.

When you are arrested for drunk driving, you will be taken to the police station to be photographed, fingerprinted and processed, and your car will be impounded. You will be given a ticket or summons to appear at a future court date. In more serious cases, you will be held until you can see a judge at arraignment to have bail set.

The DWI/DUI Arrest: You Must Comply

When you are pulled over for DWI/DUI, the officer will ask you to get out of the car. Refusing to get out of the car *can and will* get you arrested. While you have a right to remain silent, you must get out of the car when asked and must present your license and registration when asked for them.

After the arrest and in case of your refusal to submit to a chemical test, you will typically be given an administrative hearing at your state's Department of Motor Vehicles to have your license reinstated. The officer is obligated to show proper warning was given to you regarding the consequences of your refusal to take the chemical tests. If it is established at the hearing that the officer did not give adequate warning, your license may not be revoked. However, you still have to face the charges in criminal court.

Penalties for DWI/DUI

Because DWI and DUI penalties are high and conviction can have severe life-altering consequences, it is very important for you to discuss your case early on with an experienced DWI/DUI lawyer. Some of the penalties of a DWI/DUI conviction include:

- Jail time.

- Driver license suspension.

- Increase in insurance costs.

- Notification to your employer.

- License reinstatement costs.

- High court fines.

- Expensive court-ordered DWI/DUI classes.

- Installation of an expensive court-ordered ignition interlock device on your car.

- Long periods of probation.

Underage DWI/DUI – Zero Tolerance

While the legal limit for intoxication is 0.08%, for a person below the age of 21 there is a zero tolerance policy. This means:

- While it is illegal for someone under the age of 21 to buy or possess alcohol, drinking and driving under age does not require a legal limit of intoxication and ANY level of intoxication is sufficient for a criminal charge.

- For underage offenders, the charges are more serious and include not only a DWI/DUI charge, but could also result in charges for underage drinking or possession of alcohol by a minor.

An experienced DWI/DUI lawyer is essential to evaluate any sobriety test results and figure out how to challenge the results, including any procedural errors or mistakes made in obtaining them.

Like any other case, if your DWI/DUI case is not resolved with a dismissal or a plea, it will proceed for trial. The issue before the jury would be whether or not your ability to drive was impaired by alcohol or any other substance. In all states, a blood alcohol (BAC) level of 0.08% is sufficient for a conviction. However, your attorney might still be able to challenge the validity of the test results.

Deciding to plead to the charges, negotiate a plea to a lower charge (if possible) or take your DWI/DUI case to trial is dependent on your individual case and the circumstances of your arrest. Discuss the options with your attorney after he or she evaluates the strength of your case, in order to decide the best course of action.

Police are permitted at your trial to testify regarding their opinion as to whether your ability was impaired at the time of the arrest. While such testimony could mention things about appearance (e.g., bloodshot eyes, odor of alcohol or other illegal substance, slurred speech, etc.), they are not considered by the court as evidence of your impairment in and of themselves. The totality of the evidence is considered.

Plea bargaining in drunk driving cases is rare. Prosecuting drunk driving cases has become political in nature and because the safety of the community is the primary goal, many of these cases go to trial.

REAL LIFE EXAMPLE

Owen was charged with a count of DWI. At his trial, evidence was presented to establish that his ability to operate a motor vehicle was impaired at the time of the arrest. The arresting officer testified to Owen's bloodshot eyes, slurred speech, and an odor of alcohol on his breath at the time of the arrest. The bartender at the bar where Owen had been drinking and the guy Owen rear-ended immediately prior to his arrest also testified. His breathalyzer test was also presented which indicated his blood alcohol content was above the legal limit. Owen was convicted of DWI as the evidence presented supported a conviction.

In DWI/DUI cases, the type of vehicle being driven at the time of violation could increase the severity of punishment. For example, the charge and punishment is higher and more serious if the vehicle is a cab (with a passenger), certain types of trucks, or if there is a child as a passenger in the car.

DWI/DUI Convictions in Another State

A drunk driving conviction, regardless of the state in which it occurs, could affect driving privileges in another state for a period of time, if the other state recognizes the conviction. Most states have reciprocal agreements with other states, which means that they share traffic violation conviction information. The link below lists the states which have agreements with your home state:

http://www.carinsurance.com/kb/content26407.aspx

Non-citizens Facing Criminal Charges

Navigating the criminal justice system is challenging for U.S. citizens. But for non-citizens, the penalties upon conviction can bring disastrous consequences. Getting a lawyer early on is essential!

A non-citizen, even with lawful status in the United States, faces grave negative immigration consequences if convicted of a criminal offense. These consequences can include deportation, not being able to obtain citizenship, and more.

Under current immigration law, a non-citizen may be deported if: (1) convicted of certain crimes which are either considered crimes of moral turpitude or (2) aggravated felony offenses. For crimes involving moral turpitude, deportation may result when there is a conviction with a sentence imposed of more than one year (within five years of entry into U.S.). If a non-citizen has been convicted more than once (for crimes not from a single scheme), it falls under the moral turpitude clause.

A crime of **"moral turpitude"** is a crime that violates the accepted and customary rule of right and duty between each one of us. It could be conspiracy to defraud, robbery, forgery, arson, larceny, certain major crimes against the government, most sex crimes, including rape, and most aggravated offenses.

Because a non-citizen convicted of a crime of moral turpitude risks deportation, it's essential to understand the full consequences of any plea bargain.

Certain offenses that result in one or more years of imprisonment, are considered aggravated felony offenses under immigration law. This means they can lead to deportation. For example, a burglary conviction with a sentence of one year imprisonment is considered an aggravated felony under immigration law and is grounds for deportation. However, a burglary conviction with less than one year imprisonment sentence is not.

A plea to a non-aggravated offense, rather than an aggravated offense, could potentially avoid deportation (in certain cases). Your criminal defense attorney will advise you regarding which crime to plead to in order to reduce the immigration consequences.

REAL LIFE EXAMPLE

Salvatore was a lawful permanent resident of United States, but not yet a citizen. He supported himself by salvaging building materials and scrap metal from vacant commercial buildings. He was arrested and charged with burglary in the second degree, and failed to exercise his right to remain silent. Thinking he could explain his way out of the problem, Salvatore told the police that he was just trying to support himself and buy food. But these statements were incriminating and essentially constituted a confession that would be used against him in court.

To expedite the proceeding, the prosecutor offered a plea bargain of burglary in third degree (which is a lower class felony than his initial charge) and a sentence of one year in prison if Salvatore agreed to plead guilty. Salvatore's attorney knew this agreement would make the conviction fall within the category of aggravated felony, which could result in deportation. He persuaded the judge and the prosecutor to reduce the sentence by one day (a sentence of 364 days in prison) to avoid this consequence.

First Steps for Non-Citizens Facing Criminal Charges

For non-citizens it is vital to let your attorney know, as soon as possible, that you are not a citizen of United States. This information is critical in every step of a criminal process from seeking a bail application, to negotiating a plea on your behalf, to preparing for trial.

The negative impact of the conviction on your immigration status could very well change the strategy chosen by your attorney in your representation. In such cases, your attorney might not only fight for your freedom, but also for preserving your immigration status.

What to Know When Crossing Borders with Pending Criminal Charges

For non-citizens, it's important to avoid traveling across borders while your criminal case is pending. At the border, custom officers could see that you have been arrested and have a case pending, which could affect entry back in the country. If you have a criminal case that is open and pending and the border officers ask about the pending case, make sure *not to admit* to any elements of the crime you are charged with.

If your case is pending, you are not yet convicted and are only charged with a criminal offense. A charge is NOT a conviction.

Direct and Collateral Consequences of a Criminal Conviction

A criminal conviction can mean more than jail time. It can affect your right to get public benefits, your right to vote and many things others take for granted.

A criminal conviction has direct consequences such as (1) a prison sentence, (2) certain clear immigration consequences, (3) post-release supervision or (4) clear parole consequences.

But convictions may also have many collateral consequences, which are not as apparent and yet can be as severe as the direct consequences, depending on the specific case and on the specific individual. These can include: risks to employment, risks to obtaining student loans, risks to driving privileges, risks to obtaining public housing or public benefits, consequences to child custody and visitations, having to submit a DNA sample to a databank, duties to register as a sex offender and having to pay court fees and surcharges.

Indirect Consequences of Convictions

Immigration. Convicted non-citizens may be subject to deportation by the Department of Homeland Security as a result of a criminal conviction. A criminal conviction will also affect an application to become a naturalized citizen.

Employment. A criminal record may appear on a background check done by an employer.

Driving privileges. A criminal conviction could result in suspension or revocation of driving privileges.

Professional licenses. Criminal convictions must be disclosed for most professional license applications.

Suspension or ending of public benefits. A criminal conviction might have a negative impact on eligibility to obtain benefits for housing, social security benefits and eligibility to receive student loans.

Family. Depending on the type of criminal conviction, your conviction could negatively impact custody or visitation rights, or in extreme cases, result in termination of parental rights.

Below are some additional resources to learn more about the collateral consequences of a criminal conviction:

- http://www2.law.columbia.edu/fourcs

- http://ccnmtl.columbia.edu/portfolio/law/collateral_ consequen

- http://www.immigrantdefenseproject.org

- http://www.lawhelp.org

Relief From Consequences of a Criminal Conviction

If the collateral consequences of a conviction are onerous, state procedures sometimes permit a convict to get some relief.

Many people with a previous criminal conviction suffer every day from their past and experience collateral consequences after the conviction. It is important to know that depending on your state and your past offense you might be eligible to petition the court to obtain certain forms of relief.

While there are many consequences resulting from a criminal conviction, there are a few ways, after a conviction, to relieve some of the collateral consequences. Depending on your specific case and your state, you may be able to petition a court to seal or expunge your criminal record or seek to obtain a certificate of relief or good conduct. The laws allowing these petitions in certain states are designed to allow for reintegration of the offenders back into the community and for the reduction of the rejection and isolation of the offenders.

Sealing Criminal Records

In instances where your case is dismissed in your favor, either through acquittal after trial or dismissal for other reasons, your arrest, prosecution, and fingerprint records shall be sealed and destroyed. For example, if after your criminal trial the jury finds you not guilty of the charges against you and acquits you, the case is dismissed in your favor. The court should seal and destroy your arrest and fingerprint records.

Depending on your state, there may be laws on sealing criminal records even after you have been convicted of certain offenses. For example:

- Records of convictions for most violations or traffic infractions which are not considered crimes may be sealed.

- Dismissals made after completion of an adjournment period are considered dismissed in your favor and the records should be sealed.

Note that even sealed records may still be available to certain government agencies. Each state has its own rules regarding what is available and to whom.

Expungement

In certain states, the law allows you to expunge your records for certain offenses (usually first-time offenses). Expungement would remove from the public view all or part of your criminal record or would change the record of your conviction from "convicted" to "dismissed without guilt."

The laws for sealing and expunging records vary from state to state. Contact an experienced criminal attorney to learn more about the specific laws in your state.

Certificate of Relief from Civil Disabilities

The **"Certificate of Relief from Civil Disabilities"** is issued by some states and allows certain eligible offenders to apply to the court to be relieved from disabilities or bars to employment that may result from their previous convictions. However, not all states offer it.

The certificate is issued to eligible offenders convicted of a misdemeanor or one felony offense and who have shown rehabilitation. A person with such a certificate cannot be denied employment or issuance of a license solely because of his/her previous convictions. However, this certificate would not permit the convicted person to be eligible for public office and it would not mean that the conviction is pardoned.

REAL LIFE EXAMPLE

Frank was convicted of felony charges for illegal possession of a controlled substance when he was a young man. After a few years, he decided to apply for and was successfully granted a Certificate of Relief from Civil Disabilities. Frank applied for a job and still disclosed on his employment application that he had been convicted of a crime, because his attorney explained to him that a Certificate of Relief from Civil Disabilities does not pardon the conviction or take away the conviction.

Certificate of Good Conduct

A **"Certificate of Good Conduct,"** also granted in only some states, enables a person convicted of one or two felony convictions and any number of misdemeanors to demonstrate rehabilitation. Like a Certificate of Relief from Civil Disabilities, a Certificate of Good Conduct may be issued to remove all or some legal bars or disabilities to employment or issuance of a license.

While the Certificate of Relief from Civil Disabilities and Certificate of Good Conduct could bring some relief to the obstacles caused by criminal convictions, they do not in any way prevent a judicial, administrative or licensing body from relying on the conviction when making discretionary decisions as to refusing to issue or renew any license or permit.

Speak with a criminal defense attorney experienced in petitioning these reliefs to find out what options you have in your specific state to reduce the negative impact a conviction has on your life. The resource below provides more information about different types of reliefs:

http://www.recordgone.com

Concluding Thoughts

Involvement with the criminal justice system is something best avoided at all times. But if it happens, make sure you know your rights and get yourself the best criminal lawyer you can—because a lot is at stake.

Being charged with and convicted of a criminal offense can have significant negative consequences on one's life, liberty and livelihood. The Constitution of the United States and the constitutions of each of the states grant important rights, such as the right to remain silent, the right against self-incrimination, the right to an attorney and the right to be presumed innocent until proven guilty. It is vitally important to understand your rights, exercise them and protect them when going through the complex and often confusing criminal justice system.

Glossary

Adjournment in Contemplation of Dismissal: A judge's order giving a person who is arrested conditions to fulfill that will result in dismissing the case if he or she is not rearrested.

Adjudication: A formal legal process, such as going to court, to resolve a dispute.

Appeal: Request to a higher (appellate) court to review and change the decision of a lower court.

Arraignment: After an arrest, this is the accused's first appearance before a judge, where he is charged with the crime.

Arrest Warrant: This is a document signed by a judge or a judicial magistrate that allows the police to arrest a person. To obtain an arrest warrant, officers must present sufficient facts to constitute probable cause for the arrest.

Bail: Security posted to guarantee a criminal defendant will return to court for his/her next court date if released from jail while the case is still pending. Payment of bail is made made by cash or bond.

Bench Warrant: A type of arrest warrant, signed by a judge, which authorizes your arrest for failing to show up at a scheduled court date.

Beyond a Reasonable Doubt: Standard of proof used in a criminal trial. This is a difficult burden to prove as compared with the standard used in a civil trial which is typically by a "preponderance" of the evidence.

Certificate of Good Conduct: Document designed for individuals convicted of more than one crime who have demonstrated rehabilitation. This certificate may ameliorate the impact of convictions.

Glossary

Certificate of Relief from Civil Disabilities: This document is issued by the state and allows for certain eligible offenders to apply to the court to be relieved from disabilities or bars to employment that may result from their previous convictions.

Challenge for Cause: Disqualification of a juror from jury panel.

Complainant/Complaining Witness: This refers to an alleged victim of a crime whose testimony is material to the case.

Crimes: Generally refers to misdemeanors and felonies where a defendant could serve jail time.

Cross Examination: The chance to question the witness/ evidence at a civil or a criminal trial to prove that the witness is lying and/or reduce the evidence's credibility.

Deliberation: Post-trial process where the jury reviews the evidence presented and reaches a decision in the case.

Desk Appearance Ticket (DAT): Given at the discretion of the police for persons arrested for minor crimes, such as disorderly conduct. In lieu of arraignment at the time of arrest, the DAT requires an accused to return to court on a specific date for arraignment of the charges.

Direct Examination: When the prosecutor or defendant's attorney questions his/her own witnesses during a trial (criminal or civil).

Double Jeopardy: The Fifth Amendment to the U.S. Constitution that prohibits anyone from being prosecuted twice for the same crime.

Driving While Intoxicated (DWI)/Driving Under the Influence (DUI): Crimes for driving while impaired by drugs or alcohol.

Failure to Appear (FTA): A crime, also known as "bail jumping," which an arrested person commits when he or she fails to return for a future court date, after being released on bail.

Felony: A serious crime for which a sentence of imprisonment may be in excess of one year or a death sentence.

Hearing: A proceeding before a court or other decision-making body where evidence is heard and/or an issue as to law or fact is decided.

Hung Jury: When a jury in a trial cannot reach a verdict. If unanimous agreement is required to convict, and is not obtained, a hung jury results.

Juvenile Delinquency: Generally refers to a child committing an act which, if committed by an adult, would be a crime.

Misdemeanor: A less serious crime which carries a maximum prison sentence of one year or less.

Moral Turpitude: Refers to a crime which violates the accepted and customary rule of right and duty between each one of us, based on community values/standards.

Motion to Suppress Evidence: A motion brought in court to prevent evidence from being used against a defendant.

Order of Protection (also known as a "Restraining Order"): A court-issued order to protect the safety of the complainant (or a witness). It lists behavior and actions the person named is forbidden from doing.

Parole: The release of a person from prison prior to the end of the completion of a sentence which contains certain terms and conditions.

Glossary

Peremptory Challenge: Elimination of a potential juror for non-stated reasons.

Probable Cause: A level of reasonable belief, based on facts that can be articulated, that a criminal act was committed.

Remand: Holding a defendant on bail or in custody until a lower court provides instructions as to further hearings.

Stop and Frisk: Type of search conducted when an officer who is suspicious of an individual stops and pats down a person's outer clothing in search of a weapon. If no weapon is found, the search should cease.

Surety Bond: A bond posted by a bail bond company (licensed insurance company) on behalf of the accused in return for a fee.

Temporary Order of Protection (TOP): A court order limiting contact by an accused person with the complaining witness as a condition of his/her release or bail.

About the Author

Maryam Jahedi, Esq.

Maryam Jahedi is a criminal defense attorney and owner of the Maryam Jahedi Law Firm in Manhattan. Prior to opening her own firm, Ms. Jahedi obtained extensive advocacy skills in the public sector at the Legal Aid Society. Ms. Jahedi volunteered at the Prisoners' Rights Project of the Legal Aid Society in Manhattan, where she advocated on behalf of individual prisoners in New York City jails and New York State prisons on matters of guard brutality, sexual abuse, mental health and medical care.

Maryam Jahedi earned her B.A. in economics from University of British Columbia in Canada. She later earned her J.D. from Sydney Law School at University of Sydney in Australia. Ms. Jahedi is admitted to practice law in the State of New York and in the United States District Court for the Southern District of New York. She is fluent in Farsi.

About Real Life Legal™

Parker Press Inc., the publisher of Real Life Legal™ creates plain-language consumer information on legal, tax, business and financial subjects. Taking aim at info overload and legalese, Parker Press Inc. launched Real Life Legal™ in 2014. Real Life Legal™ provides practical advice, written by lawyers, to help people understand how the law works. Our goal is to provide solid, easy-to-understand information so *you* can decide whether it makes sense to hire a lawyer. Real Life Legal™ wants you to be prepared.

Available Titles

Bankruptcy Basics: Chapter 7 and Chapter 13
Marina Ricci, Esq.

Business Owners Startup Guide
Susan G. Parker, Esq. and Lynne Williams, Esq.

Elder Law: Legal Planning for Seniors
Susan G. Parker, Esq. and Maria B. Whealan, Esq.

Employee's Guide to Discrimination and Termination
Joanne Dekker, Esq.

Estate Planning: A Road Map for Beginners
Susan G. Parker, Esq. and Maria B. Whealan, Esq.

Filing a Homeowner's Claim: Natural Disaster or Not
Dawn Snyder, Esq.

A Lawyer's Guide to Home Renovations
John A. Goodman, Esq.

Available Titles (Continued)

Planning for Pets: Trusts, Leash Laws and More
Joanne Dekker, Esq.

Planning for Your Special Needs Child
Amy Newman, Esq.

Special Needs Education: Navigating for Your Child
Lynne Williams, Esq.

U.S. Veterans: Your Rights and Benefits
Maria B. Whealan, Esq.
with Paul M. Goodson, Esq.

What to Do When Someone Dies
Susan G. Parker, Esq.

You've Been Arrested: Now What?
Maryam Jahedi, Esq.

Notes

Notes

Notes

Notes

Notes

Notes

Notes

Notes

www.ingramcontent.com/pod-product-compliance
Lightning Source LLC
Chambersburg PA
CBHW060632210326
41520CB00010B/1569